sec

To Dale

To the good times
& the not so good...

Till next time—

Sin

seconds

Sid Evans

Pillar Press

*To all the barmen and maids
and those who picked up the tab.*

For Delphine…

Copyright © 2005 Sid Evans

Seconds
First published 2005 by
Pillar Press
Ladywell
Thomastown
Co Kilkenny

ISBN 0955082110

British Library Cataloguing in Publication Data.
A CIP catalogue record for this book is available
from the British Library.

Printed in Ireland by ColourBooks

10 9 8 7 6 5 4 3 2 1

'Men talk of killing time, while time quietly kills them.'

Dion Boucicault, *London Assurance* 1841

foreword

Perhaps the greatest challenge facing any artist is the exploration of the 'human condition' and, for most of us, this condition is defined by the mundane. In *seconds* Sid Evans approaches this challenge by examining the monotony of the everyday and, at times, elevating it to the epic.

In scale and ambition *seconds* is epic. It deals with the complex subjects of thought, interior monologue, half remembered emotions, discarded dreams and sets these nuances against the backdrop of time's rhythmic march.

The aim of *seconds* is to involve us in a half told, unfinished story by means of characters with whom we can empathise. The poem is set on a Thursday, on the 11th of November, Remembrance Day, in an unspecified year but it is clearly set in the modern world. The characteristic emotional content of *seconds* finds expression through a variety of techniques, from direct description to highly personalized symbolism as seen in this passage below.

> *I summoned the sea*
> *and waded out*
> *till my knees felt the foam.*
> *I watched you there,*
> *where the white tipped rose waved to greet you,*
> *and waited till I couldn't see you.*
> *And, upon seeing that you were unreachable,*
> *I summoned the horses*
> *and rode back home.*

seconds uses many processes: narrative, dramatic, aphoristic, descriptive, erotic, and personal. Throughout the poem Evans moves us from one mode to another but preserves the overall unity through the consistency of the formal pattern and a structure that, while not giving itself up easily on a first reading, is remarkably consistent and concise after further exploration. The formal patterns available to any poet vary considerably but Evans effortlessly assimilates what went before and somehow makes it new and vital.

> *I could hear the sound of recollections churning.*
> *The filament of my memory was burning*
> *beneath the coruscation of the toilets sign.*
> *Ivory-faced chessmen blinked in line*
> *between gossips and rumour-mongers,*
> *do-gooders and done-wrongers.*
> *The television, off-station, weathered interference*
> *as individual histories subsided into incoherence.*

On one level *seconds* is a naïve poem. It is naïve in its ambitions, and naïve in its scope and it is naïve in the belief that poetry of such passion and with such a deficit of irony can, and should, still be written at the beginning of this already turbulent century. The poem simply, paradoxically simply, attempts to explore three quiet, externally unremarkable lives; a young woman is reminded of her grief, a young man recalls the summer and an old man remembers other days. The microcosm of their bed-sit lives reveals more about the isolation and potential for mental dislocation inherent in urban living than the vast canvas of many an inferior novel or documentary.

Evans has demonstrated his commitment to the genre with this work. Readers who open their minds, readers who read poetry in order to try and experience what the author has achieved with the words on the page, or what he has attempted to achieve, will, it is hoped, find much to admire.

first thing

'...and darkness was on the face of the deep.'

Then there were sounds, voices came out of the darkness.

> *...Atlantic low moving rapidly northeast,*
> *expected three hundred miles north-east of Poland*
> *by midday tomorrow...*

Between the stony, blistered face, the chiselled, impassive climb and
the sea, a hard place, churned by the arthritic fingers of time, standing
on the shore in the stinging lash of the spray,
  ever wading through the detritus of castaway
    oilskins and broken radios,
      frayed knots and second-hand clothes;
        between the shards of the shattered hourglass,
          encrusted with the petrified past remnants of distraction
            and the familiar ring of action and retraction,
              counting whys, what ifs, and could've beens...
                he remembered nothing.

> *... Greenwich light vessel automatic, eleven,*
> *one thousand and thirty three,*
> *falling slowly...*

Televisual storms
over semi-detached aerials
blew in from the south-west on deep-sea swells;
eleven, one thousand and thirty three,
    over the sea, a six and two noughts,
      recycled premonitions and afterthoughts;
        exhumations of auld lang syne

of the flights and escapes that drowned in the brine,
took the scars of small deaths and the wounds beneath
the flesh,
the goings and the goings and the catching of breath
onward, downward, half a league…and so on
before all that coming back… and…
endgames and swansongs.

…violent storm eleven in the Irish Sea…

In a still and distant rock-pool
he envisaged a pair of heavy eyes
and was reminded of sleep for a moment.

Lundy, south by east seven, sixteen miles,
one thousand and fourteen,
falling quickly…

Elsewhere, the moment passed,
the colours ran away from her eyes.
And with a quiet hand, she extinguished the radio,
and turned on her thoughts.

part one

Thursday (or First Post)

Thursday, she raised an eyebrow at the demise of the moon,
and slipped from burgundy creases, a cup of tea too soon.
As night-time's tousled hair ran rings about her head
she extended a cool arm to the cold side of the bed.
With aching limbs, too early, a routinely murmured sigh,
in the half-night, the half-light cobwebbed in her eyes.

She drifted, naked, through the hallway, gave an involuntary shiver
and eyed, with dull surprise, the crack in the bathroom mirror.
Five slender fingers tugged at knotted, auburn hair
and, with a twist of the hot tap and an empty, fragile stare,
she appealed to her reflection with expectant dismay
and watched time's tiny scalpel engrave another day.

But a veil of steam ascended to rub away the score,
so she stopped counting and locked the bathroom door.
Aching amongst the flotsam of assorted pills and potions,
scented essential oils and restorative skin lotions,
she cast her mind back, to when the doubts began
and wiped the mirror with a careless stroke of an unbejewelled hand.

Cradling her head, arching her back,
stretching and sighing till the feeling came back,
she wondered how long this nausea would last
and, in a kind of liquid sleep, she stepped into the bath.

Analgesic waters embraced her blushing thighs,
soothing night-time's bruises that daylight would disguise.
Washed into demulcent drowse but unconvinced by the day,
she laid a hand upon her belly as contemplatively she lay,
underwhelmed by engagements and the jewellery of her peers,
lifestyle magazine lifestyles and cappuccino careers.

Tired of plastic teaspoons and designer bottled sense,
interactive insensitivity and artificial intelligence,
her days had paled from neon adolescence, and faded in the sun
of reckless summers and the heady excesses of a Prozac generation.
Now the bathroom window threw crazy patterns on the tiles,
of years that had shadowed her with a six-day-a-week smile.

Years that she remembered, impulsive and cash-free,
of pubs and fields and road-trips and parties on the beach
and sunnier Novembers, when the music was enough,
with a threadbare woollen jumper to keep her warm on weekends off.
But the bath water had cooled and memories blurred,
as a tiny, embryonic thought germinated inside her.

> *What is the sound of silence breaking?*
> *A pin-drop? The outbreak of war?*
> *'It's A Wonderful Life' in the flat next- door?*

But the flat next-door was quiet and she lay unaware
of the clatter of the letterbox at the bottom of the stairs.
The usual correspondence, from gasmen and debt-collectors,
speculative bank clerks and predatory tax inspectors
and a picture of a stranger shore with an unfamiliar view,
on a postcard from beyond the grave from someone she once knew.

A Note on the Breakfast table

I don't know what time it was I finally got to bed.
Nor can I say, for sure, how long I slept,
but it must be still early
and I've been up for an hour
or so

and I can't remember, exactly, what I may have said
or what promises I'm supposed to have kept
but I guess it's still early,
so I'll just take a shower
and go.

A loaf of bread and the bus fare home

Answer-phones blinked in deserted kitchenettes,
In self-contained, one-bedroomed, bachelor flats,
furnished with aborted breakfasts,
of cold tea and a half-slice of toast,
saucers and eggshells and unopened post.

In the morning fog of magnolia hallways,
forgotten keys and identical doorways,
words of reconciliation and letters of thanks
spread all over doormats on the back of a postage stamp.

The world outside had succumbed to an ordinary day.
Every other stranger concealed a familiar face
and bodies creaked into motion.

Laundrywomen frothed with television highlights
as short spin settings recycled yesterday's whites
and wrung the life out of stained cotton sheets.

Streets stretched ahead and spilled onto
pavements that shuffled under foamy skies.
Steel shutters clattered amidst market barker cries.

Dinner-ladies dished out lukewarm baked beans
in strip-lit bakelite and Formica canteens,
crackling with the nattering of cornflake deejay's.

Hairdressers dreamt of holidays
and splashed on cologne and snipped split ends,
with a sprinkle of talc and a little something for the weekend.

The park shivered peacefully and turned a page.
She stopped reading and turned away.
No one blinked an eye
as someone stepped lightly on somebody's grave.

Wrought-iron arches vaulted larger than life
over passengers bound for the 8.25,
the umbrella'd platform scuffing with suits,
a somnambulant huffing and staring at boots.

Waiting rooms spun
between source and destination,
remorse and anticipation,
under a vulgar mist
that wrapped the town in infertile hesitation.

He screwed his face to the wind
and jangled past the station
with a handful of poems and a heart turned to stone
and loose change enough for a loaf of bread,
a packet of cigarettes and the bus fare home.

Seahorses

I remember the rocks ...
on the shore ... that day ... when we were children.
I remember them then.

> *I summoned the sea*
> *and waded out*
> *till my knees felt the foam.*
> *I watched you there,*
> *where the white tipped rose waved to greet you,*
> *and waited till I couldn't see you.*
> *And, upon seeing that you were unreachable,*
> *I summoned the horses*
> *and rode back home.*

Souvenirs

In the park oddfellow sat,
overcoated beneath a browbeaten cap,
a ninety-year-old diary and the Times in his lap.

His youth in fragments, deformed by age,
he could still see in the shadow on the page,

shades of the past,
a life in miniature of lead soldiers and toy cars,
model railway commuters and a half pint of Bass.

A life left behind him in second-hand shops,
the lost glove, the found umbrella,
assorted regimental buttons in an old tin box.

Days of teacups and macaroons,
washing dishes with a few old music hall tunes,
easy listening among the ruins of Sunday afternoons.

But now had come the moment to sit and stare
at fallen leaves scattered in tranquil despair;
a birthday present of bonfire rings and the perfume of smoky air.

A moment interrupted by the burning in his eye
of searing recognition as she passed by
with a picture postcard sunset in a patch of blue sky.

Blinded by a instant of familiarity,
some half-seen reflection of intimacy;
a gesture
captured in a photograph,

a passing remark
about winter waiting at the end of the metropolitan line
and the silent tick of a watchman meticulously making time.

A familiar sound, or so it would seem,
the murmur of a rumour,
like a half-forgotten memory or a half-remembered dream.

The school bell tolled from beyond the churchyard,
the strident playground clamour began to lose its swing.

The lesson for today is about to begin.

Fool's Gold

If you had said goodbye to me,
I should have been cut off mid-speculation.
But you didn't
and I
discovered fool's gold
and corroded
in expectation.

She put down the postcard and picked up the glass.
'Looks like rain…' the barman forecast…

MEMENTO MORI

part two

seconds (prelude)

After the silence of the eleventh hour;
After the reveille
and the reawakening of a thousand fleeting recollections,
the moment hung suspended on an fragmented second.

A shadow wavered in the corner of the room,
high spirits had begun to flag.
Lips were buttoned, tongues were tied and chins had lost their wag.

Empty words, wrenched from speechless mouths,
fell silent on the bar,
and drowned in quiet contemplation
in the pickle jar.

seconds

With an overflowing ashtray and an empty glass,
he just smoked the atmosphere and drank to the past,
because clean air and a clear head was too much to ask,
when fragrant teenagers laughed, but didn't get the joke,
and old flames lingered like plumes of smoke
that sting your eyes and stain your hair
and leave that faint, sweet scent of decay in the air.

As the last cigarette burned through his fingers,
a distorted sense of urgency malingered.
The blameless started running out of people to blame
and pasty faces looked to the mirror in vain.
And the out-of-work actor read unpublished plays,
as the poet tried to remember what he was going to say.

The jukebox kept repeating itself, the telephone was broken
and the swear-tin was empty, because no-one had spoken.

And then he glanced clockwards and said, 'Is this it?'
as he took out some loose change and a rolled-up bus ticket.
'Is what it?' asked one, 'Is this what?' said another;
'Why?' said a third, as a fourth said, 'Why bother?'

Three o'clock slunk by, making excuses,
too late or too early to be of use,
but nobody noticed and fewer cared.
The one-eyed oddfellow just sat and stared,
winding his watch to watch the seconds unwind;
not so much dying, as killing time.

An air of degeneracy wafted like stale after-shave
over the architecture of sedentary lives,
where Modigliani women and fugitive dreamers
exchanged fictional childhoods embellished with lies.

Thus the afternoon stretched out, stale and unquenched,
with that familiar sulphurous stench
of burnt poetry & spilt confidence.

She stopped next to him and leant on the bar,
smiled weakly and showed him the postmark.
The card bore the dog-eared smears of neglect
and he handled it with care, as a mark of respect.

She said she was tired, she didn't sleep well last night.
'I'm half sick of shadows…' she sighed.
She gave him a cigarette, he gave her a light.
Her hand brushed quietly against his arm.

She pressed a piece of paper into his palm.

'Do you ever get that feeling that something's about to happen?'
'And then it doesn't?'
'Yes.'
'Yes.'
He nodded, she sighed.
He noticed her face, her eyes,
her hands; the same slender fingers and nails as his own;
two hands, silently, clutching at bones.

'I was thirty yesterday and you gave me pearls.'

Her words, when she spoke, weighed the world
but when she fell silent, colours filled her eyes.
Immersed in their own insignificance
they watched the bubbles rise.

'Shall we go?'
'Go where?'
'I don't know'.
She paused.

They sat for a moment, contemplating…
'I guess it's all in the waiting.'

Easter was early this year
and summer came late.

We didn't have time to…

You cut me off before I even started.
You never even asked me what I really
wanted.

Together, they waited, with big autumn thoughts.
'…I think we took summer for granted…'

She slipped away to pour the wine,
gliding gracefully in time
with the music of her sadness.

4.07

She had trudged too many miles around this bar,
he'd been adrift in a world too long
for either to make sense of where it all went wrong.

He'd spent too long finding the words,
she had no words left to dispense the blame
and words were all that remained.

But these shadows persist, absent by design,
bruises of hindsight, not discoloured by time.
The blue-black permanence of the desolate letter
that stirs up another by-the-fireside upsetter,
the ghostly trace that wound about her finger,
an enduring reminder
of the numbness
of the unmentionable injury
from the undiscovered country.

Eighteen odd months since he'd shuffled off,
with not a bang nor a whimper but a muffled cough.
An incautious overdose of barbiturate and wine
induced by bad debts and borrowed time.
He had watched himself dissolve in the glass
whilst all around him lost their heads;
a knowledgeable fool,
unadulterated by others' realities.
Death is, indeed, a very serious injury.

In her own acquiescence, she deigned to admit
that her remaining silent seemed as odd as talking about it
to all those who were in the know.

'There's always someone to tell you when it's time to go.'

5.24

The rain rinsed the street with glum resignation.
A pair of Alka-Seltzers ordered rum and coke and fizzed with
 indignation.
Forlorn suppersingers and backpayers of rent
started counting out the hours and days they had spent
coming to terms with squandered moments
in the cold sweat and beers before lunchtime.
'I've been doing it for years...' he said to his friend,
'I take a bit longer these days, but I get there in the end...'

Someone started a conversation with, 'Did you see..?'
and sobersides and chinadoll sloped off for a pee.
Has-beens, nearlies and the never-were
started telling stories they'd already heard.
The barman, polishing glasses with faraway eyes,
Looked to the clock with unsurprise
as six o'clock quietly passed away.
My God, how the seconds seem like days these days.

7.31

Perhaps this time he had gone too far.
Idly watching the grains scatter on the bar,
he poured salt in the wound that leaves no scar.

And the summer sand
and the sea,
the ring and the reason.
And he, beguiled by tantalising season,
watching, waiting
for a moment of truth,
the silver band
buried in the rocky playground of their youth.

And last night, such a sudden outpouring of grief,
 dark muscles, clinging in fragile relief
   to a thin residue of summer
     on the arms
                    and thighs.
           And an awkward silence of reusable lies.

   Stretching, destitute, twisting limbs
 arching in the solemn comfort of a remedial screw,
 the clenching breath and furtive *I love you,*
    a macabre dance beneath a troublesome moon.

       The night was not for talking in an empty room.

  And now the answer was discreet,
   in black and white,
 folded twice, on a crumpled till receipt.

9.11

Somebody laughed, the charity box rattled.
Televised bedlam flickered on the breeze.
The room was still filled with inconsequential prattle.
You could see the oxygen amongst the pleasantries.

10.19

Oddfellow took out his handkerchief,
blew his nose and rose to his feet.

Standing at the bar,
 the whisky trembling
   in a gnarled hand,
          he suddenly burst out singing.

               All at once, frail thoughts stirred
                and memories flooded
             the space between the words.
     Eyes that had spent too long gazing at the sun
   stared through the smoke and saw their reflection.
Blue streaked yellow wisps stroked the faces of nicotine-stained pictures
  who stared back from the grave at the congregation,
     as strange as ones own face, as alive as another,
         ingrained in the imaginations of the next generation…

         The words chipped the veneer and weakened the crowd,
            the very fabric ripped,
   the seams came apart in a feathery cloud…

I became weak and things began to drift.
The joke had worn thin and the air became stiff.

I could hear the sound of recollections churning.
The filament of my memory was burning
beneath the coruscation of the toilets sign.
Ivory-faced chessmen blinked in line
between gossips and rumour-mongers,
do-gooders and done-wrongers.
The television, off-station, weathered interference
as individual histories subsided into incoherence.

Someone was bound to break sooner or later
to the expectorative spit of the percolator.

The waves again came crashing.

The bulb in the toilets sign is flashing.

10.55

I can't wait any longer for the sunlit days,
holding my breath for the next best thing,
a few moments before the onset of spring.

And yet, there are other days
when the past beats at your back,
when reminiscence turns to black
in the torpor that blows chip wrappers around
the drizzled promenades of seaside towns.

Stepping through the endless flotsam and jetsam
of damaged sentimentalists who don't want you to forget them,
entrenched in the wake of other peoples lives,
doing what is required, just to survive,
in a small room with a window and the smell of coffee,
a commemorative mug and a Flanders poppy.

But I am tired,
on a broken seat, staring at the floor,
the smell of urine and graffiti on the wall;

'Give me the time of day and I will give you the time of your life…'

How long does it take?
        I can't do it anymore…

There's a ripple of applause as I reach the door.

Tired, tired,
longing for an outbreak of silence.

The song was timeless but the singing had been done,
a dismal stagnancy engulfed everyone.
Boredom set in as the panic abated.
The nervous energy had dissipated
and the only sound that quickened the room
was the wretched tapping of someone navigating the gloom.

A mute, unending yawn swallowed every living thing,
even the alcohol had lost its sting,
the clock, itself, seemed to have lost the will
and, for just a monochrome second,
                              everything stood still.

A great deal had been said,
too little to be remembered
and much more than could be understood.

I had no idea what it could possibly mean.

Her eyes fixed mine with a meaningful stare,
"Why can't it just not mean anything?"

But she went on waiting on people she'd never met,
remembering things that she was trying to forget.
The poet still tried to impregnate the pause
with a borrowed anecdote and second-hand metaphors.

The painter explained why he would no longer paint,
the gravedigger made peace with argumentative saints
and all those other people that you never spoke to,
gathered upon the shelves
and watched with suspicion

and talked amongst themselves.
Still the landlord vacillated with consummate skill,
with an eye on the ladies and one hand in the till,
and at half past midnight he called for time,
for it's time we all want, but we haven't the time.

And by four in the morning, the passengers had fled.
The insomniac watchman had gone home to bed.
The legless, the harmless, blind drunk and insane
laughed the last laugh and walked home in the rain.

The undertaker just smiled and took out his tape-measure
and handed round his card and said, 'Come see me at your leisure.'
But oddfellow in the corner did not stir,
his crossword completed except for one word.

Remember you will die;
no more time wasted
after the initial moment of doubt...

And stillness smothered him as the lights went out.

part three

Last Post

Now the door had closed on another yesterday
and left her in the silence of night-times hallway.

Here she was, home now,
and she didn't know how she got there.

> *And was this really it,*
> *these four walls*
> *and a few words scrawled on a rolled-up bus ticket?*

And yet, from time to time,
these moments, like fragments
shattered deep beneath the skin,
opened up the cracks in her life
and the light come in.

The hallway ticked,
the pipes moaned in the gloom,
murmuring rumour like the radio in the next room.
And, as if the feelings inside her had grown,
had matured unawares,
she put the number by the phone
and quietly climbed the stairs.

epitaph

This is the time of our lives.
Was it worth waiting for?

Those who are gone, dance lightly through the ages.
No more days of wasted journeys,
or uncertain tomorrows on empty pages.

And, for all the other unfinished days,
just cleaner windows and cleaner sheets,
a long untravelled road,
and another chance to get some sleep.

The city breathes with an iron lung,
heaving heavy metal on asthmatic breath
in the small hours, going on…

Past memento moris inscribed on the pavement
and past lives screwed to the wall,
spray-painted scenes of bereavement
in subways and town halls.

And on through cardboard catacombs,
where the nowhereman lives in nowheremen's tombs,
with methadone and meths to account for their deaths
and obituaries in the brims of their hats.

And on through corridors and alleyways
marked with the fingerprints of all our yesterdays.
Across iron bridges and along railway tracks
that carve destinations beside chimney stacks
that spit the fumes from the last dying embers

of a tribute that only the river remembers.
Graveyard shiftworkers look to the sky and strain to hear
the night shudder as dawn crosses the weir
with a monoxidised cough and a methylated laugh;
almost audible, the engraving of a neglected epitaph.

He walked through the city
beneath a telescopic sky,
with folded promises in pockets of change,
in search of something rich and strange.

And sometime he would feel fingers knotting into his
and he would feel the fondness of her kiss.

and so on…

and he walked onto the shore
and breathed the air
and heard the song…

      I've been here before

       And when he returned to the city, it was still going on.

Post Script

Thus, the road rises to meet us, from time to time,
but we all go back in the end.
And the second hand retreats,
then beats over again.

And the night is filled with night-times noises
and darkness is on the face of the clock.
Obscuring hands
and disguising voices...

                I wonder when they'll stop.

Notes

part one

A loaf of bread and the bus fare home

line 24   *a little something for the weekend*: Gentlemen's barber shops used
           to offer contraceptives to their clients.

Souvenirs

line 1   *Oddfellow*: a member of a fraternity similar to the freemasons,
           founded in the 18 century.
           (source: *The Oxford English Reference Dictionary*)

part two

seconds (prelude)

line 2   *reveille*: pronounced 'rivalli' – military waking signal on
           bugle, played at the end of the two minutes silence on
           remembrance day.

seconds - *1.46*

line 20-1 Sartre, *La Nausée* (Friday):
           Three o' clock. Three o' clock is always too late or too early
           for anything you want to do. A peculiar moment in the
           afternoon. Today it is intolerable.

seconds - *9.11*

line 2   *bedlam*: Bedlam was originally the popular name of the hospital
           of St Mary of Bethlehem founded as a priory in 1247 at
           Bishopsgate, London, later becoming a mental hospital.   In
           1815 it was replaced by a building in the Lambeth Road, now
           the Imperial War Museum.
           (source: *The Oxford English Reference Dictionary*)

<u>seconds - *10.19*</u>

line 6   Cf. Sassoon, *Everyone Sang* 1919
          (see also seconds - *11.27*, line 1)

<u>seconds - *10.28*</u>

line 1   Sartre, *La Nausée*

<u>seconds - *11.27*</u>

line 1   Cf. Sassoon, *Everyone Sang* 1919:
              'The song was wordless; the singing will never be done.'

line 7   Cf. Edvard Munch's diary (describing *The Scream*)
              '…it was if a mute unending scream pierced nature…'

line 34   Cf. *The Band Played Waltzing Mathilda* (Eric Bogle) (from the
          album *Rum, Sodomy & The Lash* by The Pogues)

line 40-2 (7,4)

part three

<u>epitaph</u>

line 3   Cf. Edward Thomas, *Roads*:
              'Now all roads lead to France
              And heavy is the tread
              Of the living; but the dead
              Returning lightly dance…'

line 42   Cf. Derek Walcott, *Omeros*:
              'When he left the beach, the sea was still going on.'